D0772271

THE SEVEN WONDERS
OF THE MODERN WORLD

CHICHÉN ITZÁ

BY SARA GREEN

BLASTOFF!
DISCOVERY

BELLWETHER MEDIA • MINNEAPOLIS, MN

Blastoff! Discovery launches a new mission: reading to learn. Filled with facts and features, each book offers you an exciting new world to explore!

BLASTOFF! UNIVERSE

GRADE K

GRADES 1-3

GRADE 4

This edition first published in 2021 by Bellwether Media, Inc.

No part of this publication may be reproduced in whole or in part without written permission of the publisher.
For information regarding permission, write to Bellwether Media, Inc., Attention: Permissions Department, 6012 Blue Circle Drive, Minnetonka, MN 55343.

Library of Congress Cataloging-in-Publication Data

Names: Green, Sara, 1964- author.
Title: Chichén Itzá / By Sara Green.
Description: Minneapolis, MN : Bellwether Media, Inc., 2021. | Series: Blastoff! Discovery: The seven wonders of the modern world | Includes bibliographical references and index. | Audience: Ages 7-13 | Audience: Grades 4-6 | Summary: "Engaging images accompany information about Chichén Itzá. The combination of high-interest subject matter and narrative text is intended for students in grades 3 through 8"–Provided by publisher.
Identifiers: LCCN 2020018879 (print) | LCCN 2020018880 (ebook) | ISBN 9781644872659 (library binding) | ISBN 9781681037288 (ebook)
Subjects: LCSH: Chichén Itzá Site (Mexico)–Juvenile literature. | Mayas–Juvenile literature. | Yucatán (Mexico : State)–Juvenile literature.
Classification: LCC F1435.1.C5 G74 2021 (print) | LCC F1435.1.C5 (ebook) | DDC 972/.65–dc23
LC record available at https://lccn.loc.gov/2020018879
LC ebook record available at https://lccn.loc.gov/2020018880

Editor: Betsy Rathburn   Designer: Brittany McIntosh

Printed in the United States of America, North Mankato, MN.

TABLE OF CONTENTS

DESTINATION CHICHÉN ITZÁ!

Welcome to Mexico! Your first destination is an ancient Maya city called Chichén Itzá. The drive from your hotel passes several **cenotes** filled with water. People often stop to swim!

EL CASTILLO

A guide meets you at the entrance to Chichén Itzá. He shows you the sites and explains their history. The highlight is the city's most famous structure, El Castillo. It was built to honor a Maya snake god named Kukulcán. The pyramid rises 79 feet (24 meters) into the air!

AN ANCIENT CITY

THINK ABOUT IT

Why do you think the Maya chose to build Chichén Itzá where it is?

Chichén Itzá is an ancient Maya city. It is on the Yucatán **Peninsula** of Mexico, near a small town called Pisté. Chichén Itzá covers about 4 square miles (10 square kilometers). The city is surrounded by a thick jungle.

There are no rivers or lakes near Chichén Itzá. But an underwater cave system stretches beneath the city for hundreds of miles in every direction. In some places, the ground opens into cenotes. They were the main sources of water for the Maya people.

WHERE IS CHICHÉN ITZÁ?

CHICHÉN ITZÁ
MEXICO

N
W   E
S

CENOTE

Most of Chichén Itzá's structures are made of limestone. This hard rock is common in the area.

ONE FOR EACH DAY

Each of the four sides of El Castillo has 91 steps. A final step at the top makes a total of 365 steps, the number of days in a year!

The city's largest structure is El Castillo, a large, four-sided stepped pyramid. It stands in the center of the city. Nearby, the Temple of the Warriors is another large, stepped pyramid. It is surrounded by 200 stone columns. A statue called a **Chac Mool** guards the top of the temple.

CHAC MOOL

9

EL CARACOL

Another impressive structure is an **observatory**, built to study the planets and stars. Inside its tower is a spiral staircase. The staircase inspired Spanish explorers to name the observatory *El Caracol*, which means "the snail" in Spanish.

10

Further away, a *tzompantli*, or skull rack, shows off detailed carvings of human skulls. These were likely part of religious ceremonies in ancient Chichén Itzá. Near the skull rack is the Great Ball Court. It is almost twice as long as a football field! Here, people once played a sport with a hard ball. It is the largest ball court in **Mesoamerica**!

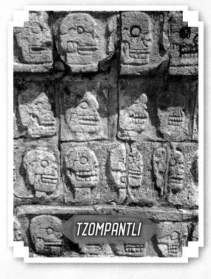

TZOMPANTLI

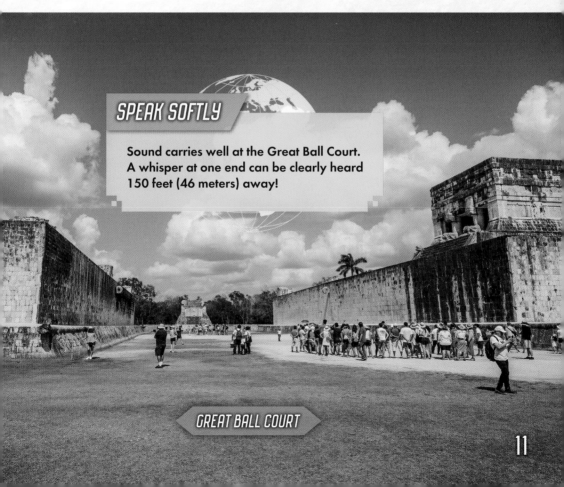

SPEAK SOFTLY

Sound carries well at the Great Ball Court. A whisper at one end can be clearly heard 150 feet (46 meters) away!

GREAT BALL COURT

WATER AND STONE

The ancient Maya began settling on the Yucatán Peninsula around 2500 BCE. Chichén Itzá was first settled as early as 250 CE.

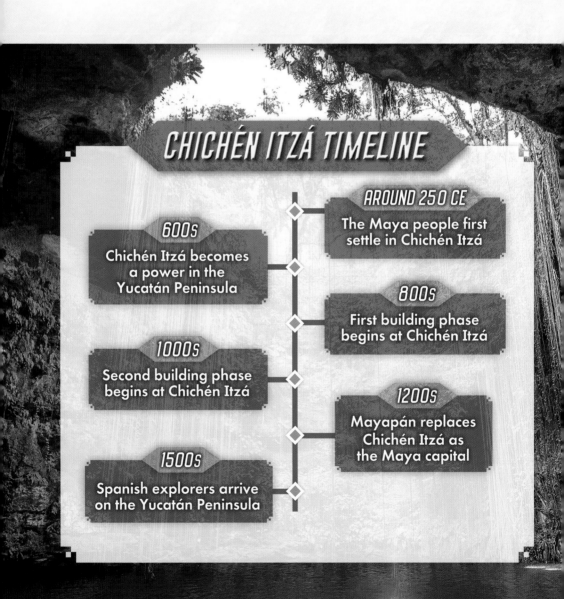

CHICHÉN ITZÁ TIMELINE

AROUND 250 CE
The Maya people first settle in Chichén Itzá

600s
Chichén Itzá becomes a power in the Yucatán Peninsula

800s
First building phase begins at Chichén Itzá

1000s
Second building phase begins at Chichén Itzá

1200s
Mayapán replaces Chichén Itzá as the Maya capital

1500s
Spanish explorers arrive on the Yucatán Peninsula

SACRED CENOTE

Two large cenotes probably drew the Maya to the area. The cenotes were dependable water sources. They may have served a religious purpose, too. The ancient Maya believed cenotes were gates to the underground world of the gods. The Maya tossed offerings such as jewelry and pottery into the cenotes to ask the gods for rain.

Chichén Itzá was an important political and economic center by 600 CE. Many grand structures were built in the city during the next 600 years. But building was difficult. Workers did not have wheels, pack animals, or metal tools.

Workers crafted tools from stone. These were used to dig limestone from a nearby **quarry**. Limestone pathways called *sacbeob* were made to move materials. The workers rolled the blocks to the building sites on logs using these paths.

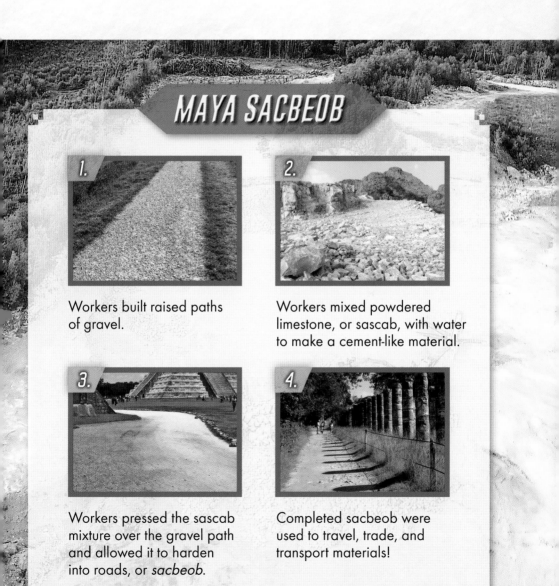

MAYA SACBEOB

1. Workers built raised paths of gravel.

2. Workers mixed powdered limestone, or sascab, with water to make a cement-like material.

3. Workers pressed the sascab mixture over the gravel path and allowed it to harden into roads, or *sacbeob*.

4. Completed sacbeob were used to travel, trade, and transport materials!

LOST AND FOUND

By the mid-1200s, power on the Yucatán Peninsula had shifted to a city called Mayapán. Nobody knows exactly why Chichén Itzá declined. Many historians think a long period of dry weather was to blame.

Chichén Itzá was abandoned by the time Spanish **conquistadors** arrived in the 1500s. They claimed the city for themselves. It became a place to graze cattle. But the Spanish did not consider the city important. Over time, the jungle grew over Chichén Itzá's pathways and structures. Only the locals remembered that it was there.

SPANISH CONQUISTADORS
ARRIVING IN MEXICO

MAYAPÁN

THINK ABOUT IT

Why would dry weather have driven the Maya from Chichén Itzá?

In the 1800s, explorers John Lloyd Stephens and Frederick Catherwood visited the city. They were the first known explorers to make detailed maps and drawings of Chichén Itzá.

An American named Edward Thompson bought the rights to Chichén Itzá in 1894. Thompson **excavated** the ruins and **dredged** the Sacred Cenote. His finds included carved jade, gold, pottery, and other treasures the Maya threw into the well. He also discovered human skeletons. They were probably the remains of human **sacrifices**.

JADE PENDANT

DIVING FOR TREASURE

In 1909, Edward Thompson dove more than 60 feet (18 meters) to the bottom of the Sacred Cenote to search for treasures.

EDWARD THOMPSON
DREDGING THE SACRED CENOTE

19

THINK ABOUT IT

Why do you think the Maya built new structures over older ones?

JAGUAR THRONE
INSIDE EL CASTILLO

Excavation of Chichén Itzá expanded in the 1900s. In 1931, a team of researchers discovered an older, smaller pyramid within El Castillo. This discovery was not surprising. The ancient Maya often built new structures over older ones. A red throne shaped like a jaguar was found inside this inner pyramid. Its spots are jade stones!

Experts recognized the need to **restore** ruins as excavations continued. Both American and Mexican teams uncovered and rebuilt ancient structures. Researchers also made maps of the area. This helped them better understand how Chichén Itzá developed over time.

THEN AND NOW

THEN

In the 1800s and early 1900s, concrete was used to rebuild crumbling structures. But the material was not historically accurate. It also damaged structures.

NOW

Today, specialists use *bajpek*, a special cement, to restore structures. This cement is similar to what the Maya used. It will not damage structures!

VISIT, LEARN, AND PRESERVE!

Today, Chichén Itzá is one of the most popular **tourist** destinations in Mexico. Millions of people visit the city each year. Chichén Itzá was named a **UNESCO** World Heritage Site in 1988. In 2007, it was named one of the New Seven Wonders of the World.

COMPARE AND CONTRAST

EL CASTILLO

GREAT PYRAMID OF GIZA

LOCATION
Mexico

LOCATION
Egypt

YEARS BUILT
between 800 and 900 CE

YEARS BUILT
between 2580 and 2560 BCE

MATERIALS
small limestone blocks

MATERIALS
blocks of limestone and granite

ENTRANCE
top of pyramid

ENTRANCE
bottom of pyramid

PURPOSE
temple for Kukulcán

PURPOSE
tomb for Egyptian ruler

Many tourists visit Chichén Itzá during the first days of spring and autumn. During this time, the setting sun casts a shadow onto El Castillo. It is said to be Kukulcán. The shadow moves down the north side of the pyramid to connect with a stone head at its base.

Scientists are still making discoveries at Chichén Itzá. Each one teaches them more about the early Maya.

In 2016, researchers used **imaging technology** to look inside El Castillo. They knew about the hidden pyramid discovered in the 1930s. But they were amazed to find an older pyramid hiding inside the larger two! It was likely built between the years 550 and 800. It may be one of Chichén Itzá's original structures!

EXCAVATION AT CHICHÉN ITZÁ

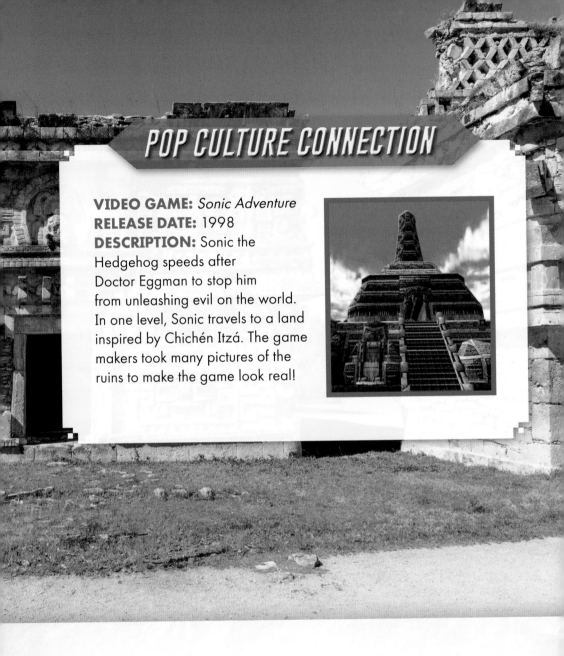

POP CULTURE CONNECTION

VIDEO GAME: *Sonic Adventure*
RELEASE DATE: 1998
DESCRIPTION: Sonic the Hedgehog speeds after Doctor Eggman to stop him from unleashing evil on the world. In one level, Sonic travels to a land inspired by Chichén Itzá. The game makers took many pictures of the ruins to make the game look real!

More exciting discoveries followed. In 2017, researchers used **radar** to locate a tunnel system beneath Chichén Itzá. They went below ground to make maps of the tunnels and caves. Some were underwater! The researchers studied the flow of water to find areas that were hidden for hundreds of years!

In 2019, researchers discovered another new room beneath the city. Inside, they found dozens of bones, jars, and other **artifacts**!

ARTIFACTS

CAVE BENEATH CHICHÉN ITZÁ

27

Chichén Itzá's popularity has a downside. High tourist traffic threatens the fragile structures. Today, climbing or entering the structures is not allowed.

The city faces other threats. An underground river flowing beneath El Castillo makes the ground unstable. Some people fear the pyramid could collapse. **Acid rain** also threatens the ruins. It **erodes** surfaces and damages **inscriptions**. Experts seek new ways to protect the city. Their efforts will help this wonder delight visitors far into the future!

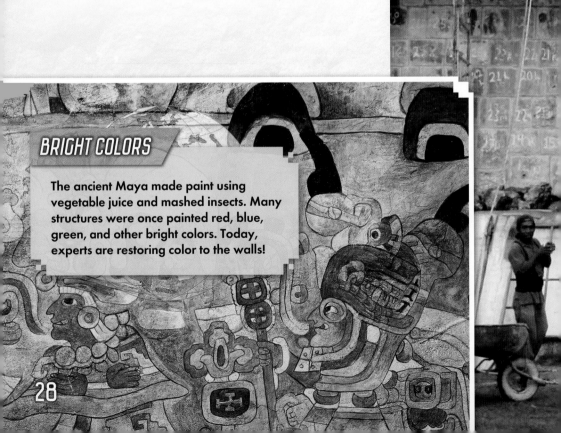

BRIGHT COLORS

The ancient Maya made paint using vegetable juice and mashed insects. Many structures were once painted red, blue, green, and other bright colors. Today, experts are restoring color to the walls!

RESTORING CHICHÉN ITZÁ

GLOSSARY

acid rain—rain that contains chemicals from pollution; acid rain can damage buildings.

artifacts—items made long ago by humans; artifacts tell people today about people from the past.

cenotes—deep holes in the ground that are often filled with water

Chac Mool—a form of Mesoamerican sculpture; Chac Mool shows a reclining figure with its head turned to the side, leaning on its elbows, and supporting a bowl or a disk on its chest.

conquistadors—leaders of Spanish conquests in the Americas during the 16th century

dredged—removed materials from the bottom of a body of water with shovels

erodes—wears away over time; erosion is caused by wind, water, ice, or human activity.

excavated—dug out

imaging technology—a technology that uses radar to find and take pictures of hidden objects

inscriptions—letters or words carved on something

Mesoamerica—an area stretching from modern-day Mexico to El Salvador

observatory—a place for studying stars and other objects in space

peninsula—a section of land that extends out from a larger piece of land and is almost completely surrounded by water

quarry—a place from which rocks are dug for use in building

radar—a device or system that sends out radio waves to find objects

restore—to return something to its original condition

sacrifices—offerings of something valuable to please the gods

tourist—related to people who travel to visit a place

UNESCO—the United Nations Educational, Scientific and Cultural Organization; UNESCO recognizes and protects World Heritage Sites that have cultural, historical, or scientific significance.

TO LEARN MORE

AT THE LIBRARY

Green, Sara. *Ancient Maya*. Minneapolis, Minn.:
Bellwether Media, 2020.

Kule, Elaine A. *Exploring the Ancient Maya*.
Mankato, Minn.: 12 Story Library, 2018.

Tyler, Madeline. *The Ancient Maya*. New York,
N.Y.: KidHaven Publishing, 2019.

ON THE WEB

FACTSURFER

Factsurfer.com gives you
a safe, fun way to find
more information.

1. Go to www.factsurfer.com.

2. Enter "Chichén Itzá" into the search box
   and click 🔍.

3. Select your book cover to see a list
   of related content.

INDEX